JOURNEYS

POEMS AND SEQUENCES, 1997 - 2010

ROB STANTON

Newton-le-Willows

Published in the United Kingdom in 2022
by The Knives Forks And Spoons Press,
51 Pipit Avenue,
Newton-le-Willows,
Merseyside,
WA12 9RG.

ISBN 978-1-912211-88-3

Acknowledgements:

Poems and sequences appeared (often in different forms) in: *Fascicle*, *Great Work*, *Noon*, *Octopus*, *Poetry & Audience*, *Salt, Shampoo* and *Stride*.

Wells I, II, III and *Bresson:* L'Argent appeared in the chapbook *Trip-* (Knives Forks and Spoon, 2013).

Many thanks to all the editors involved for their support.

All quotations in *Bresson:* L'Argent taken from Robert Bresson, *Notes on the Cinematographer*, trans. Jonathan Griffin (Green Integer, 1997).

Epigraphs for *The Middle's* taken from Shelley's *Prometheus Unbound* and John Ashbery's 'The Handshake, the Cough, the Kiss' respectively. Heading quotations in *The Middle's* are taken from Gustave Flaubert, *The Dictionary of Accepted Ideas*, trans. Jacques Barzun (New Directions, 1954).

Contents

III. Sequences, 2005-2010

I. Sequences, 1999 - 2005

Provenance
(*a narrative   in mosaic form*)

[an invocation]

a call
on heights
         (*– these*
church-tall trees –
               their spires –) …

i. arriving

[an image]

a nub
      of
sand   clenched tight inside
              his fist

[a root]

containing

sun   (– *its*
seed –):   the

mind   through stone

[a covenant]

yes: this

completes
us: *this*: this

single   word

[a source]

left

    face
to
    face

       we
lie
    beside

      the river …

ii. testing

[an intimation]

penumbra –

shading

hope, pro-

leptic, odd

[a defiance]

this

      dancing   on
all fours;
        this

joy   of beasts

[a fulfilment]

our
   wings
adopt
     the air:

            we
swerve   away

[an observation]

it
  sees
      us
here: *the word-*
                contorted
light

[a culmination]

so –
       brimming
pestilence –
            sky
               wrestles
                    earth …

iii. settling

[an equilibrium]

new life (– *a newer*

dust –): torn

from (– *brought to* –)

[a bond]

our questing

tongues; our

perfect exit-

wound

[a clearing]

some
        breeze

                to break
                        sparse
branches
            out
to air

[a construction]

our Crusoe-

proud response: *"we*

made   it

home"

[a home (*for david and jo*)]

(– a place you

carry to, carry

between –)

[a legacy]

we stoop
          to
keep
      the scene
immaculate

Rob Stanton

Vast Shadow That

I.

Vast shadow that
you can't perceive, but know
is there. A wood
crowded with more
than trees. The rains begin, ever
so faintly.

II.

Uneasy introduction, framed
by leaves. An awkwardly-expressive
praise. A blessing, formed,
like snow, to dissipate. My second
thoughts have had their second
thoughts. That look that gives secrets away.

III.

Just look at this,
will you? Or do you seek
distraction? Love? A party? Some
new friend? I'd place this book
into your hands myself, but for the wear
and tear. A simple plot. A ploy.

IV.

Had had to go. No other way.
The business occupied so
little time. The natural growth
had shown the peace of mind to
turn it off, but yet it
stood, an audience to your whim.

V.

Yet another season, piling up – but
this one was my friend, so off I went,
dodging the brickbats of the lesser
clones. My innocence returned. So too
my guilt. There is no room for further
days, or love.

VI.

This? That? A choice between
not two replies but of
two fates. A candle gutters and
blows out. A single act of
grace, of guestly charm. What do
these questions mean, the harsher ones?

VII.

Reading in this world, its
contoured rills, you find that loneliness is
happiness, that gestures
of reproach reel lovers in. That net,
the overture, is over. Waves
that crash & spread & echo back. Are gone.

VIII.

First person
narrates. A long delay
to hear that song. The martyrs
are unique ones, holding off
the coming end. A distant sound
of gunfire, intermittent.

IX.

An enforced sense of closure
makes your day. The pen
dictates our moods. The moon
inclines. Something to nothing
in
a nanosecond.

X.

Me here, where I
belong, horizon-bound. Darkness
makes visible
a fenceless tract. The larger
box enshields our
wherewithal.

XI.

A secret so
obvious nobody
notices. A turning
away. A dark shade at the plant's
heart. Something seen
in a book somewhere.

XII.

Dig in, against
the roots, uproot
the tree; let blood flow, sap-
like, through the grass; upend
the blades, then
darken them, blunt scourge.

XIII.

Accept this resignation, take
on board: this journey
ends in homestead
ennui, ever. Crowds on-
look, as is their wont.
Nothing goes on.

XIV.

A trust placed in the self
alone. Let light – it
penetrates the room's
odd gloom. A bawdy
sign – unsuited, not
unwelcome – up in smoke.

XV.

A love unspelt, unset, lolling
about; a name unsought
that must be caught, and primed.
Lithe (it shuttles forth) emptiness (it
sheds its skin). Saying is knowing on
this happy sphere. Your own reflection, poised.

XVI.

Middle age, usurping youth,
conspires with its own
longings, curt and cute.
A step beyond the frame
belies the frame. The footprint
yields its truth, upholding-star.

XVII.

Self-disassembling, art, your
sky is seen, your bluster feigns
the weather, is
itself. Your destiny is
lied to, at the gate. The inquiry
will linger, over facts.

XVIII.

Barmy, in
a summer sense – not
private, not illegal, but
in love. A synchronicity
of disappointment, sad. Forget
the winter's tang, the poem lulls.

XIX.

Encapsulated in
the human bleat, he passes
from all knowledge. These, his
songs, will mourn
for him, be whistled, snuggle up. The
bank is steep, the river dull. Dull sweep.

XX.

Disposable, so not
discernible, I whimper
on – the
elements my friends, the weather
not. Continuing
to sing, as furniture.

XXI.

Recycled mind, put to
best use, milk time, and
offer produce up
once more. A prison
is no prison without
locks. A breath of air.

XXII.

Reflection doesn't count, being
itself. That average light, at
end of day, its pockets of disturbances
and calm. Stretch out your
consciousness until it warps,
then harvest your responses. Pin them down.

XXIII.

Town/country mouse, where do
you go, passported and embaggaged to
the hilt? A temporary jaunt, in-
elegant, expressing all your
passiveness
at once. You'd better hide.

XXIV.

Yes, I endorse
your product, daily
sun, and would write advert
jingles, if I could. My jutting
angles give resistance
up. You scrape on by.

XXV.

The poem as
a comfort blanket, torn, and
thrown away by hapless
parents, torn, and mourned
by bandy children in
a glade. It never works.

XXVI.

Tall buildings, flattened
life, bulging
with pride. No self-
concern, flinging about
in style. A tourist's eye
setting the scene to limits.

XXVII.

After the pets'
escape, she rambled on, a
country belle transduced to
city life. The painted trees
succumbed to grand
despair, their only way.

XXVIII.

Not day. Not night. Nor
dawn. Nor dusk. Bad
light: it darkens up the
vast expanse, confuses
mountains with their valley
pals. Sidereal calm.

XXIX.

Desiring desire, the looks
of others, girls, I went
back to the cave to claim
my lyre. The individual was
matchstick-strong. Bald night
came on, without another note.

XXX.

The repetition led to
variation; the bedtime
story lasted past
the dawn; the state religion
dropped theology; the case
was cracked.

XXXI.

Bible stories like
a cartoon strip, the wrath
of God mere slapstick, back
and forth. We *clamour*
at our desks. The office
shakes. We wait in state.

XXXII.

The map produces
goosebumps, futures
pursed. Our youth
will not return, nor will
our age. The cars
depart. Their windows form our cage.

XXXIII.

This could be the last
time, I
don't know. The first time
was a gas, a prophylactic
jet. The next time begs.
The middle sags. And yawns.

XXXIV.

The sound
of surf. Your thinking dies, subsumed
in music it
was born
to hear. You
peter out.

XXXV.

A child's life is its
toy, is circumscribed; its
root the middle
way, it stumbles
on, a movie jogging
back towards its cause.

XXXVI.

A house,
in thought; in
actuality, a garbage
can. Black night
slinks in, at home, your
double, pent.

XXXVII.

Please
trust me, I'm
your one way out
of here. You never know.
The shoestring budget
stretches to your dress.

XXXVIII.

Buy One Get
One Free. Twinning
process, yielding up
dead cells. You wake
too fast, forget yourself, and weep.
Your name is on my lips. On everything.

XXXIX.

An effort being made,
excessive force. Nature's
crucible
of working. We (its
slaves), paid handsomely, paid
off, affront.

XL.

The body and
the soul are parting
ways. A fork. Beyond it, there,
unhanded dark. Complexity
will shrug its well-
built frame, then shirk it off.

XLI.

Our lives are largely seen, but still
ignored
by those who make the difference, those
in power.
As widows of ourselves, we'll
pay their fare.

XLII.

Confrontation scenes
bring me to tears. The alley
grows to boulevard
proportions. There,
beneath the beach, we'll
grow our home.

XLIII.

Something expected;
something denied: a thing
that pivots time, directs
our dreams, that we,
perched on the precipice,
can't hear.

XLIV.

A time of sluggish
work, of peeling
skin, of blisters
on the main-frame, of
a lack. Send
food. Or help. Or both. Don't pass us by.

XLV.

Nose twitching, like
a rabbit's, bundled up, you fought
your way to day-
light, underground. Now, over-
heard, you plummet
to your height.

XLVI.

Climate bears its
outer face. Our days –
planted with evil signs,
with dodgy weather – spurt.
Nothing collects the debris.
That is all.

XLVII.

The suburbs and the outskirts
know the drill. But you
don't – you must learn it
over time. And time, a
daisy chain, refutes
you yet.

XLVIII.

Pausing at the station
for a train, the man is asked
the question
of his life. He blurts his
answer out; he turns
his face, and smiles.

XLIX.

Works
and days. The nature
of the universe. Lips. Lapse. No
easier, life
putters on. It
chafes.

L.

A gesture of farewell, of
greeting, both. Your patience
falters, time
its downfall,
love. The shadow lingers on. In
prone position.

Novel

i.

None forgotten first a look
gone bad significance itself considered
book. Entitled time a penance
due, completed pretext a competent
meaning under words, a new

copy. Things found, a copy
from work foisted rack volume
none forgets, first mover moved
a scribble gained, recorded here
uninsipid moment emptied earlier here.

ii.

Utterly distinguished canonical hour: nine
times over animal vegetable natural
echo deus fortified Venus dominates
back forth emanating spirits vehicle
past sense, there misery impedes

frequently: ego dominates us: ego
purged – lone name, lone nature
proleptic new hurt, nine times
over video hurt – she spoke
suns, soul rules, fixed stars:

precession ends beginnings tired procession
unaltered, chambers music hearts pulse
trembles. Earlier passions actions sent
backwards eastwards back and forth
then ghostlike weeping hearts minds

eye. Beginnings end most noble
bliss wracked wretched pleasure – 'here
come bounds' – many-times-sought borne dignity
imaged godlike – mannered, governed – hierarchy
stricken perceptual, most profit bliss

reasoned pleasure: image spoke truth
lacquered, copied, imagination-powered, attended to,
found full her 'one and
only' name – by many messed
around – a third degree, a

larger claim: eye-forming, eye-mitigating, eye-
delighting master often hindered here.
A twelfth degree appeared to
deign a domineering of said
market forces, a certain decorating

advice – inceptive light not nine
times over circled back a
larger claim, an often hindered
master – 'here *are* bounds' – commanding
to seek, found out promise

to himself self-uttered truth, truth-uttered
self speaks parts to wholes, whole
speaking parts are tethered, rendered
necessary dressing up, around, a
nourishment attended to, age-suitable: a

civil self inscribing headings: reasonable
advice as counsels profiteers, ill-theming
strand a fond and sudden
amateur attachment ten miles down.
Omit much to see more, a

third degree of heat mines
eye – beginnings end – consulted ends
proscribed ('she had secrets' – but
of this no more is
said). At moment of enactment

recognition butts forgiveness into line:
foreknowledge renders innocence enough, donating
Venus echo deus fortified dominoes
animal vital natural: omitted before
sense importance lies utterly distinguished.

iii.

Fear of beginnings saw him
coming: locomotive power to motion
place to place to boss
intense: moved on to do
so by desiring treatments pending

language gender matches maker, foxhole-
dwelling, seeing psalms – processional – arrayed:
a baseline bassline vivid, vital:
voiced echoes clamour in a
desert, parted from needed decorum

can't even endure purpose, expectant
faces awaiting answer: something which
cannot fail. A dab and
splash. An anxious speech a
presentation stayed: addressing pleasures spoken

Rob Stanton

to tantalise gently another tantalised
bare: ego tampers, centres circles,
opens stimulation and modestly inhabits
circumstances apart from automatic nonsense
(bliss now lies: words that

praise respond to questions, to
truth-telling condition-distracting intentionally-composing
nonesuch words:
shame equals departures forever spoken
otherwise). Resolved to choose material
graciously one decision undertaken theme

loftier than air can hold –
a thing in itself distinct.
All truth false in this
intellectually determined bodily substance: possession
furthers still a motive revealed

far later on, voluble and
verbal three in one that
silence speaks preceding indications concerning
her condition, never again addressed
to her directly: occasion for

new theme offers listening pleasant
as brief concerning possible love
mentioning laughter also characteristic: man
of men, of human vernacular:
a clarified discussion suits a

purpose understanding ancient times vernacular –
other nations happened still. Greater
poetic license conceded a blow,
composing verses more and less
the same (moved on to

do so: saw him coming:
image-coloured words fitted and resonating,
spoken to inanimate objects seen
possessing sense and reason each
together). Mighty bells see bulwarks

preserving hate – multi-roaming & tame,
indebted to civic arms – damned
duration, fill up yr temper
preternaturally stimulated: why, O voice,
translate per view – attending to

sight is a sick, sad
and dolorous menu – toss again
while labour explores options and
mighty labels fasten us in,
view the core of us.

Although appearance learnt secret hearts
gathered certain enjoyed company, knew
well each seen swooning fortunate
guide addressing pleasures spoken otherwise:
many ladies laughing themselves: stood

before gaining confidence, footnote to
desire: many ladies themselves laughing:
anxious speech a presentation stayed.
Unreal dreams more real than
urgent undressing-like retreats from social

upset: seeing and wishing to
make it evident: a telling
to enact a further part:
so gracious no attachment may
alleviate – a deviant detachment seeking

best: a better bet bites
bitter on the upsurge, caking
fit alignment on its perch –
the two preceding parts define
a curve, a new recruitment

to a further cause, disposed
to influence sufficiently: to miracle
a past back to that
time. A shorter space no
mortal might attest: here space

alights: a slave to machinations
fumbled up, a will to
rant, a power. Intense transfiguration
says itself and seldom leaves
oppression *to* itself: appearance fascinates

division, first in reason (company
not yet explainable to different
subjects popping up announced and
falling back) relates by love
a proposition made by reason's

bough: a heart's condition examples
pity's place, a comfort torn
by blanching face, to eyes
destroyed and never seen again
by anyone, addressing nothing: set

him up and saw him
off: essential theme loftier than
last: feared beginnings booked: a
vital accident in substance setting
up a secular departure formulating

iv.

an empty city widowed great –
involved improved and called and
empty yet. Why moderns said
it solo: civility itself plenty
popular – facts still quasi-seen, dominated

gentle in this, in that
text: preface denies conclusion its
seclusion, the manner in which
it should be dealt with:
discussed departure, greatest reverence, empty

yet. A triad of excuses,
reasonable intentions denied a visible
capable absence, insufficiently commanding, a
wobbly grip: its nine appearances
deceptive unreasoned occurrences, numbers played

a role pertinent to theme
blameworthy in the extreme, an
overbalanced top, to number her
closer: fitted in unaided orphan
topics fitted up: a count

begun by soothing her most
worthy soul (in moving heavens
perfect relationship): just one reason
one asks another another reason
why number might multiply harmony,

movement affect the earth, following
relations of this to that –
she and number are actually
synonymous, actively accompanied by three
more subtle persons (pleased us

more): we plainly see: a
nine, a miracle, a root.
Infallible truth a paradox makes
understandable more subtle thinking: perfect
numbers digit up to a

reckoning: movement affects the earth:
a century placed in a
century accompanied by three: a
nine, a miracle, a root:
substance not sunrise calendars require

touching ten times ten the
moving heavens: a perfect relationship
turned barren city, all departing
hence shocked, stripped of dignity
weeping still: those in, concerning

our condition: in: how modesty
edits the soul, civilising plainer
facts: and on: an explanation
excuses attempts at pithier turns
of phrase, following the front

serving said material as face.
Wish it so, someone: reproach
gets gloom words follow, written
in rough, hinging on understanding
contrary to the saying of

rights: auditors pass go as
ever: entirely here and printed
down: a perfect relationship accorded
to said reckoning: we plainly
see it: *cities sit solitary*.

V.

See revolutions caused first mover
moved, familiar source a moment
uninsipid – sentence pressing down – knowledge
hers: ask after us, gazing
upon a full stop *coup*

d'état (unique apparent aim an
elevation – span granting span – a
flourish seen). Anti-ironic muscle-bound gazette
resolves its paper confines too
abject: too often surplus energy

sees off revulsion: a picture
pressed concerning pitted page on
page – light upon light – a
surge implicit improves precession, choirs
appear as ominous, secular benedictions

bias bliss, a basis ached
forensic, set apart: ask after
us: one hoping simple pleasured
soul named graciousness ascending ladder
bliss (*best book battered better*).

Rob Stanton

Leaper

leap or laugh
in summary   retreat
in broken bottles
recall   senator malignant
parts the water
here pierces there
sand melting sand
in three eyes

inaugurate debacle   body
follows shadow fallow
ranger me &
my semi-detached abutment
forests of Europe
clawed memory   flame
herds pain   sequestered
body follows shadow

awe or ore
densely packed multitudes
summoned back rebarbative
oil ails alibi
soiled spiel sanctifies
one more time
summer imagines winter
sight gets sight

exact blurb capitulates
tell me anything
fake garb plus
gadget plus one
needlessly provoking weekend
assured power crumples
three little words
really quite gone

yeah like right
proportion emptied out
amplitudinous   calling forth
full knowledges crimes
broken to know
man the monarch
visible prospectus extricating
follows you down

rattlesnake rattlesnake make
her mine break
mere gait as
fast as you
can   voice forming
tea taken   lines
make noise   con
-firm   -fine   -demn

-serve   -trite   -tact
tribe answers questionnaires
that dangerous mess
taking depositions   making
statements   pulling   apart
nothing but sea
between   limp lights
another fine performative

either ether   garden
is illuminated   in
visibly   taken aback
sanguine wistful physical
word buttoned up
marks on paper
without sun with
out labours neighbour

islands like scattered
rubber leaves   body
films over   grim
and benevolent so
they say   sequestered
as repressible as
heaven leaps hell
one by one

fits and starts
untenable   or so
they say   coloured
amid both white
writes black   death
of possibility reveals
much to do
sense echoes rule

rule-bending sense-echoing dependence
swallows pride entire
under mattresses spoke
sandwiches crazy paving
utterly *wanna beer*
star astringent form
science emerges fatter
science attempting winter

effort turns up
body turns up
hard as rock
stanzas interrogate hole
expected emerald impossibility
calling fish fish
rambunctious sorts these
here be woe

knee high in
discarded effervescence   reality
TV   goes limp
in plastered Paris
uplift   clasp   cast
grab   glance   and
other important frames
damned stupid things

another fun proposition
getting the ghost
together again   departing
say it ain't
sheep roam aloft
sea to shining
seam   extinct   never
in this world

in this word
insurgents requiring math
guile   gumption   drive
substance books illimitable
deserts see deserts
copious laughter embraces
everything   straightforward oxymoron
arcane   attack   avalanche

Rob Stanton

Lumber

plea ply played
offensive on scattering
notes bounced off
outlandish waiters waive
assize   a standard
bleak alarum sounds
composing scandalising bluster
unprepared   advantage axed

familiar shorthand reservoirs
abundant florid angles
remarks on present
coordinates overshadow remarks
beating the air
light vitality lapsing
straits appearing   nobody
regathers limper limbs

neglect will kill
all but weeds
inner open hidden
fighting solipsistic shy
rejoinder lights alive
debilitating love replacing
labour   demons detonate
weeds choking someplace

obeyed aubade a
hopefully inanimate *trauerspiel*
lush more subtle
quidlibet gone together
gleek upon occasion
carping space reconfigured
somewhat more opulent
literal tobogganing togetherness

smoke structures sculpture
community of one-offs
inoffensive product dangerous
perpetual war-room confidence
buffed up packed
protein narcissism takes
in maths useful
for forcing preponderance

correspondence fallacy unearthed
admit her mute
amaze   arise refulgent
friendly fire music
turns rawer bullet
ballet   flavours retort
raw biscuit mix
apologies evicted   plain

dental lace gannet
officially in shop
stopped momentous gravitas
surfing contingent toothache
round the block
imperative mood remains
mysterious celebrity apartment
ninefold insistence minefield

public savants reboot
lonely architectural boom
Disney concert resounding
hyaline presumption terminus
sticky public liberty
holy dead labour
labels vans dreams
taking trees endlessly

words grown large
exponentially lovely splurge
to hear exchequer
professing pleasures enough
to approximate artistic
endeavour   senses weather
many tiny insights
accompany a purchase

yanked into presence
one-eyed tunnel-visioned single-minded
smiling animal whole
hung pig   a
perfect grammar underlies
how trust devalues
they write several
weapon in hand

wit can shine
precarious spectacle over
reliance on light
children draw perceptions
orblike generates receives
edition onomatopoeia own
thaw mellifluously stolid
dwells on autumn

successive operatives assert
fervent critical work
pedantic & demoralising
mobbed dubbed motley
film   superfluous anatomy
actual textual presence
puddle ducks paddle
registered trade marred

baby sun redoubled
tooth & eye
delights in acquaintance
tripartite beatific smile
adds its impetus
durability attends articulation
sigh goaded tipped
snow matrix unforgetful

clothing burial reel
estate   *forever o*
enforce it   doubt
gifted credo cento
out wilting sunless
earthy paradise not
please note the
other way around

eyes ate us
inundated blind elsewhere
our millions strew
firm reproduce their
likeness either or
ore ether both
for bother both
ears hear repeats

Rob Stanton

Sequel

i.

Undisclosed unnatural knowledge natural yet
impossible: brainstem distortion abets a
sinkhole susceptibility, crowding out (and/or
into) loyal familial support always
unreal – ungrateful? – sweeping up the

enervating new. New broom new
antinomies (abuzz with fecund reasonings
this spring – foundational, elastic) testing
trials: characteristic dispositions vividly alive
albeit finer altitudes attained (untimely

dress most natural of artificial
forms): respect for painting nakedness
self-substance: frivolous leisure wasted on
the subject. Pat. Untouchable narrative
numbers rustle, undisclosed disaster rolling

faster, welling up to furious
namesake, neater peaks: each weak
example limps right off, a
hinge deploying skinnier realities (induction
less than reason, more than

nothing: process freezing time a
stuttering taboo, an intersection sold
awry) – deft, listen to a
total season run right off
a burgeoning adaptation of a

leaf (soiled senseless shift apparent
in an aftermath scenario only:
dehydrated presence as much a
Romantic resource as anything we
make it: worked from copy

twice repealed – beating oneself one
arrogance, stroking another – that old
drink/drown dichotomy): complex meeting complex
crabbed deduction: *hapax legomenon*: no
men clatter your devalued tongue

divided into minute reasons why:
dissension schisms sects, disputes a
spire, leap unto death: acknowledged
less than reason more than
timing. Pat. Theme turning in

upon itself: an elevation apparent
in an aftermath scenario only
(under-interrupted, stun: tool being, toy
with urge to play: stone
paper scissors: body coin, coin

body: a lumpy childish tongue
unravels under a hyperventilating wind,
an inundating rain): fatal writing
gets the gun: darkened light
(pure reason's) elaborates doubts good

grief (endless room for improvement,
litigation – invisible in finding – swarm
knowledge virtue property – process the
usual enemy – yapping inadequate metaphors
new flightless bird – arrival stymied).

ii.

End end; begin begin: fish
ferret fracture: stuff posterity: natural
intrusion replicates sun: fly by
green woes: agape: jaws open
to it: game-play potential. Self-made

conducting paradox useful power termed
desperate appraiser charms father away
again (spineless attachment derivation: whimsical
interpretation begging off, an infinite
diversity attained: unlike events no

second thing, no parsing-pulse – consume
by date as per objected
stance). Account for acrid moultings
of the mouth; break face
on the news. Malformed edition

preaches pedagogy by default, a
mere rapprochement gliding off: throughout
this tortured system tortured syntax
(ownership requiring taste, taste replicating
ownership: form ain't enough: rules

unimportant frame: aired bodies not
abstraction necessarily – formal displacement no
subplot subsumed *in toto*: direct,
present, stationary) entering the cannon
head-first: features of any significant

animal spirit added to the
pot (or plot: nature drives
to school, where death appears
at last. So *fucking* lame).
Habit drives shield, alignment seeking

fit, parodic mastery a gesture
past: the rest mere matter
of transcription turned intransitive: our
man infests mere symbol made
to be. Textbook overlays nook. Tears

very blood, neck prick, the
rest makes light horrendous pathos
privacy possesses ear alas his
heir apparent lives still lives
(undisciplined worker maddened scientist, cliché

central not a detour – half
its half, bound – making its
play for you: non-predatory interpretations
'honest'). Pat dynamic metamorphosis. Grand
mother, father, smug allocation appreciates

accretion, sun traverses a diverse
inheritance, approaches appropriation cowering in
the figurative – a *knot!* a
talking point! a *post!* – a
quarter maimed (squirrel's sudden shadow

implicit criticism: economic truth no
houses held). A rich boldness
needed (hurting the more by
not hurting). Pleasures profit. Balances
stay. Letters beat upon. Fatherly

engendered malady organic conscience, horror.
Letters beat upon. Grown old
in one. It is all
up. Commenting one to one,
renewed in inward health, life

demonstrating life usurping majesty – privacy
clearly seen, described elsewhere. We
must inhabit here: a proper
water container: mystery craft profoundly
clear instruction – one day knowledge

sits right in time, life
inappropriate cushioning – recalls across paper
a lasting store, kindness sharper
than hatred – lie down here
with evil, prepare for sapped

enjoyment, erratic flight: slavishly follow
mischievous possessive science – examples forever
to hand, distinguished hindsight – doctored
self moves fake ships out
of harbour – easier touching wills

all sorts: remarkable wound reproof
of friendship: stab and cure
one illness. Pat. Un-linear cycles
cause/affect, let down absorbing auto-
matic wealth (or faith) general,

tentative. Fed envious wisdom level
thread: a light dam made
from memory – un-trivial switch: see
self ugly, a much more comprehensive
fool cut down, that whole

mass. Words only game. Temple
face entered difficultly to boost
apocalypse mainframe, errors evoking emotion
even ended, spectator's lifeline flickers,
flinches. (Never wrong, right? Examples

don't abound. Wisdom's complete system
impulsive difficult light: non-graphic accuracy
itself telling: fastidious sick animal
overdoes oneupmanship. Tap. Scarcely seen
fall prevents a stumble (*soldier*

on) – false judgement positively assaults
self-ignorance: impossible aim a culture
cured in self: not just
just: just not just: edited
exemplar acts according to a

loaded place in line: each
mood contagious page contagion word
perched on the tongue corrosive,
tasty: reader, set aside and
go that way. To that.

iii.

Wow knowledge lets fly gasping
past the flagpole pulling up
to long grass sporting its
stuff: rupture on departure, glancing
off (illegible this whorl, a

real advantage, zero toll; a
home core neverending overload). Idiot
buoy, hop on a coach
and see a statue bred
in circuses. A nerve refusing

to message. Next stop sounds
cacophony: effective form from mirror
held aloft: a hell not
yet believed in, montage lacking
syntax, passion – irony-held in context's

exuberant charm – chamber on chamber
elicits no direct or final
judgement. No wiser (moth) for
having swallowed words worm detoured
here through memory. So there.

iv.

Hey, wait: we garden a
detachment, sort a shield, let
nature take its course – a
guilty crime unique unpleasant happiness
in snatches: over-bright and curious

food – moved, loved, seeking, sought:
no two-toned toneless tone – a
nightingale (mature) calls standard nesting
sound. Purged juice. Nice victory
on victory. World, with singular

projection interiorised by all, to
seat a million (softly-spoken poet
speaks of friendship selflessly framed,
haloed, in a field of
light): all thinking ears encounter

otherwise heard: paid pet a
thousand rows, collapsed laws louder
than progress: impossible (finally) to
stay close. Deaf system symbol
dead: hear me hear no

feedback. Main gust internal tree;
each next is said. He
is it. World, turned to
wound, would cure itself, tempted
to reflection; ear to office;

voice to censor. On car-door
appearance, Thales looks disconsolate ('*because
there is no difference*'). Sonic
point of view: art, apt,
announces turntable distraction, set: full-time

music niggles timeless – advice gives
way to pleasure largely: tap
a patch of ash, air
uneasy music; lack of perspective
equals perspective: hyperbole suits revolution

courting essential form the 'old
age of Alexander'. Code anxiety
baroque common sensual apparatus. Deviate
excess overflow, distract and distracting
certainty, thrust. A ruin. Proud

little ellipses footnotes folded into
anthology (sounds claps heavy raindrops
dual responsibility/leaves). Air taken in-
operates agenda, simulates discussion frantic.
Worldliness. Precision. Impact. Pulse deeper

past muster lively solid against
music one long recurrence (sly
foe found miserable). Avoid, pursue
impossible variety, imp: imagination veers
insatiable: an apt voice pierces

through: clothing rains unsingable stuff –
untypically real enunciation hurts/fragments: ten
paces mental hygiene slack at
the teat: plunge even into
yielding – *habits better curious* – mirrored

declaiming difficult enough: one latter
starter rifles sample bare. Would
not dissemble. They will not
always clap. Would sympathise. Would
fain feign pain felt over.

V.

Eat shit & run; husband
cropped hours to tread disassociate
needs; concede to breaking. Awkwardly
digesting distended proportions too lowly
earthly heights to frighten angel/beast

dichotomies (demonic states and greater
minds): stilted steps away from
selfhood folly: rapture common measures
trespassed past – immortal mortal fantasises –
knowledge, fitter pleasures, proper use.

Catchment

(a narrative   in mosaic form)

[a catalyst]

sun   in   at

the eye

provoking

love

(&

shame

i. experiment

[a summons]

news   o   masterly   its

daily   throb

[an inventory]

its

objects,

trinkets,

pleasures,

saturation

[an insight]

platonic form

(say

inward sun)   in-built

[a premonition]

an

atmosphere

of

hesitation

caught

[a fact]

nutritious
rain
  supplies

      the
backdrop
rose

[a heartbeat]

its

unseen

    trickling

        counter-

          damning
pulse

ii. hiatus

[an obstacle]

peer

moon

over

the earth   and at

the sun

[a tableau]

the
      lyre-
less

head
    the
ache

    the
       hearing

stones

[an overview]

delight-

      shapes, darkness-

shapes un-

earthly forms

[a contrast]

limbo

is

  like

    the

fast lane is

to this

[an identification]

tide-tired

moon look

askance turn

our way

iii. restitution

[a directive]

stand   out

      in   harshness

on

    a sunny
day

[an application]

the span

      between
          that

measures   measures
up

[a request]

alphabets

of
happiness

    give

her her
prize

[a perspective]

the
    stillness
of the light

rushing

from stars

II. Lyrics, 1997 - 2010

Choral-Interior

Our
music
never
suffered
Babel:
we –

alone –
must
stumble –
tongue-blocked –
into
noise.

Rob Stanton

Ekphrasis

(*Lucifer 1945*, JACOB EPSTEIN   *for Eric Langley*)

Emasculate

angel – you

                step

off air

into

        the plunge

of your own will

                    (– *defined* –

as god

'defined'

            himself

as he spoke us –).

Myth

Our
mother

sun. Our
father

moon. Both
rise.

Rob Stanton

Reciprocity

(*Elohim creating Adam*, WILLIAM BLAKE)

This
fingered-
wound defies
katharsis: we

re-
forge our
bond: we wear
each other's eyes.

Lowenmensch

It
is in
this: magic
implicit
in

the
act of
forming shape:
the lion-
men

sniff
air, trace
blood – a stiff
and final
art.

*

Stock
figures
hunt the wild –
the blooded
kill –

no
further
use, no thought
intact in
them

(*see*
lack of
memory
as blessing,
boy).

Reconstruction

Fed: sated: sapped –
mouth swallows
mouth. At dawn

a guest departs.
A vision,
honed, remains.

'Unlost, consolable; un-
fought for,
won.'

*

One
hand. The
other. Poised. The right one writes.

– and
after, left, you

cradle
to your brow   one

beautiful, unnecessary one.

Rob Stanton

Reading Proust in the Launderette

Everybody here is washing his or her second skin.

Everybody acting accordingly.

The washers' and the dryers' doors a little like windows onto
the souls of spinning clothes (these hitherto-
unsuspected souls, provoked, perhaps, into such
constant rehearsal of disturbed, circulating
consciousness – this *clothing-consciousness* – by us, as
audience, sitting in a row, observing them).

*

Marcel is taking Albertine to dinner.

*

Stitched, irregularly, into the world, you ponder *plot*.

You ponder *theme*, you ponder *character* (expressed through
clothes, expressed through manners, looks).

*

Might read the book forever, having time.

Commentary

(for Eric Langley)

Origins, beginnings which we expect. *Potentia*. All breathing
or air becoming something like the breath breathed
into. Almost an arrow shape. Source image. Makes

sky sky and earth earth. Lovely reinvestiture. Allowed
completeness. Calmly getting stuff done. Just smudging
boundaries perhaps. Distinctions further blurred.

Brackets here are happy containers too. Happy
sweeping beasts. They are their own spires. Lamps
which hung down into otherwise airy space on big

long chains. And then one moves. Almost nudges me
into thinking that. Often find myself quite useless in
the real world after. What I feel is a conflation. Kind

of tactile space. Contains the whole thing
in a small place. Is a single word lonely? Seems to live
alone a bit. Halo of the eclipse? Some short

shot of pastoral. This nubbed problem. Everything
now seems to be slippery. I earn some mercy. I abject
bow. I'll give myself a talking to as I scrub up

and brush teeth. Try out a few normal sentences. Give it
a new, more pleasant tenor. We will get ourselves
a nice rock, a diamond. Fine and delicate. Said better.

Rob Stanton

(after Heraclitus)

the sun's   as
broad as   a man's
foot

Blind Spot

Late sun; elongated shadows
of equidistant bushes, an outhouse (its
shadow stretches right across

the field). Verticals
and horizontals. Peace. Vague tremors
in the branches

of the trees, just barely nods. The
road beyond, its heavy traffic,
static in the light. There is no war.

Rob Stanton

Erratum

(found poem   for Dominic Williams)

The
next to last
sentence
on the
bottom
of page
7 should read

"herself
by letting
rooms.
In 183-
7 when Henry
Wadsworth
Longfellow, the"

Go

without.

Form
& void.

Firm-
(arm-?)

a-
ment. There

was. Apropos
light. Night;

day: divided.
Good.

ii.

Sprinkler
system

on. Nostrils. Life
as sinusitis. Verb

requiting
noun. This whole

land. "Dress it."
Sure.

'Surely'
as corrective.

Rest
as 'sanctity'. Her

inner
echoes

unto
his. Meat. Meet.

iii.

Good
for food. "Open

your eyes."
Loud-

hailer: *hey!*
That given

gave. Short
circuit? "One

of us." To
whom? In

aprons?
Skins?

Dust.
Dust. That first

evening.
(Turning

every
way.)

Ready? Re-
do.

Rob Stanton

Commentary

(for David Stirrup)

Best left on paper. A soft spot. Anti-narrative. A fairytale figure.
      Tries but
resolutely fails. Stayed in idea form. *Liked* disharmony. Thought it
      would be harsher!
'I don't believe in the artist as exceptional person.' One often
      stands alone. Eye

for beauty. Frank. Constrictive. Nevertheless fun. Off the cuff
      oddness. I
was surrounded. The only one of mine. Images rather than
      stories. Works
and titles. The skeleton of an angel. Riddled with risks. With a
      baseball bat, swiping

at traffic. Dogs will eat anything. Hugely over-exaggerated.
      Pleased it bothered
you. Denial and stupidity. *Is* the sum of its parts. The point is I
      have put them
together. It parodies mine a little too much. Destroys the more
      serious. This is not

me! Slightly puzzling. A snapshot. Sight *and* insight. Joy in
      violence. More dark
pools. A firm believer. Fond of the idea. Jar with the tone. Alack
      and alarum! Art
about art. A rich kid. British equivalent. Laurel *and* Hardy. About
      playing. Opt

for a better form. There are many other methods for seeing the
      moon shake.

Sun, Not Shift in / Natter Quicker

sun, not shift in

set to strike

solvent, altered

saint alike

*

natter quicker

uliginous

fame, the wanted

latent fuss

ex

body
wants
harsher

extra
finesse
extrapolates

pouts
per
aeon

Cat Gets Mouse the

cat gets mouse the

violence of justice nothing

to your sobs replete

the night along repast

Rob Stanton

Three Images
(after Gerhard Richter)

1. Apfelbäume
1987
Oil on canvas
67 x 92 cm

If you could only correspond
the 'out-of-focus' effort worked up here,
distorted by your own errant perception
– blurred further by hay fever's thinner tears –
with such pronouncements as
'for basically painting is
total idiocy', a more compelling picture
might emerge. As it is, you're lost: that sense
of near-simplistic *longing*, fed
through high-art thinking, flecks of red;
blue unremembered hills here photographed;
eye deadening mind, becoming screen,
hotline to pleasure: desire to just lie back
in longer grass somewhere in view of trees.

2. Apfelbäume
1987
Oil on canvas
72 x 102 cm

Just a beautiful thing, and only just
acceptable as a result: a painting with
'no meaning', and a nature 'always
against us' (apparently): these apple trees
that bear no sign of fruit ('moronic, in-
artistic'); softer, brighter light; increased
distortion; sun-haze ineffably nostalgic,
summoning up a childhood never spent
near trees like these, with time to
stop and look; hill-tiers ascending to
soft-focus heaven: and here, below,
inhabiting time like one who has to go,
varnish like ice above a deepset world,
the intellect a parasite latecomer.

3. Apfelbäume (Skizze)
1987
Oil on canvas
62 x 83 cm

In fog or under water: either way
impassable terrain. The middle ground –
reduced here to a bargain made between
some whale-like shadow ominous because
unruffled by the poppies underneath – a
uniform surface – and what's become
quite imprecise: a noise
of interference coming through. The path is
now a tease. Dark patch at road's end. Menace
unearthed, holiday snapshots revealed to be
delusion, gone awry, withholding all
so hesitantly promised: need to step
into a space depicted, breathe some air
untainted by the perfume of the real.

History Painting

Imagine stabbing that moth through one wing. Watch
its epileptic dance round that fixed point. Cast
shadow yourself over that battering shadow.
    (Are we innately cruel? A fatuous

    question. Are 'we' 'innately' anything
    at all?)
                   I let the moth, somnambulant and
dazed, escape out through the window, propped-up prop.
I didn't even have a pin to hand.

*

A white and modern space. A conference
on ethics. Professors fling their wilder gestures
out, and seem to be on edge and quite at home. The fence

is never comfortable. Neither is doubt
(a vacuum that breathes in as 'we' breathe out:
that darkness in which old masters placed their figures).

Rob Stanton

Perfect Day

perfect day
for looking
at concrete: sun

unanimous
& clouds
no recompense

Lit

'It's like one of your flats' – said of Edward Hopper's interior *Sun in an Empty Room*, 1963
– overheard at Tate Modern 28/07/04

Three stages. First: transcendent
white, bolstered by all corners
of the spectrum, divines that threshold.
Woolly foliage spurts beyond, a difficult
plateau. Triangled sky no source. A pane
unaltered.
   Second: parallelogram, skirted
heavily though lightly touched, a
yellow inhabiting brown. This is the
middle ground, where room exists, the useful
part.
   Three: deserter, skulking on an out-
skirt, leaning in; complexion uneven, green
encroaching yellow. Awareness is not
change. This is your human condition: sifted, shifty;
compromised and breathing in its alcove.

Rob Stanton

Colophon

(*Cornelius Gijsbrechts, c.1630-c.1675*)

Overview. Minutiae. The soul
and its accoutrements, brought off. The peel
reveals the workings
to be not.
          Uncanny brushes.
                   A litter of letters
poised. A *vanitas* of *vanitas*. A trip
from science down to hunting, hunting
down. Replacement king's performing seal;
the dagger's depicted detail: dead things
rendered deader; crucifix nails for hanging
equipment. Vices beaten up behind
cabinet glass. 'Nothing more is known
after this date.'
            The penknife lodged in pinewood
does not pierce;
            the backside of the canvas
is not blank.

Known Unknowns

(for Rae Armantrout)

Moth's pivotal
State of
Emergency rewound

Engrossing, penetrating –
Not entirely
Unlike play

<>

<>

Sky the
Colour of
Bruises opens

Names names,
So to
Speak, punitively

<>

<>

With everything
Figuration nothing
Elides perfectly

Undulant snake,
Urging itself
Upon itself

<>

<>

Lilac night
Pinned on
The moon

More truly
Valid dreams
Of reprimand

<>   <>

Even a   Debunking easy
Just reward   Comforts one
Is degradation   By one

<>   <>

Tone-row of   Legion of
Oaks stops   Flies declaring
One short   Trashcan heaven

An Errand
(for Susan Howe)

ox	see
headed	ax
angels	seesaw
<>	<>
incubus	insurance
arquebus	pens
erebus	caution
<>	<>
humanities	frequent
late	ecstatic
field	smallholding
<>	<>
zeal	weapons
prest	found
differently	music

<>   <>

here   acephalous
after   heartbeat
permanence   wanton

<>   <>

words   air
swerve   mere
target   timbre

<>   <>

himmel   blacksail
shimmer   topsoil
grammar   youward

That Individual
(Adorno Variations)

What's the good

of this
stripping action? A clearing

away
of the clearing

impulse. This very
debate has an antique

ring.

*

*A high
crag &*

*plenty
of ammo.*

*

(Anger

*forms the
user, hurts*

the usage.)

*

What
is it

pitches

path at counterpoint
to path?

*

Impulse.

Impetus.

Impasse.

*

The only
other voice

we aren't
arises.

From this
stems paralysis.

*

That
irritating dirt
that

fails
to make
a pearl.

*

The windows yield

four un-
distinguished, in-

distinguishable trees

&
building work.

*

Like chess where *all*

the pieces
have resigned.

Rob Stanton

Case Study: *Poussin*

(Les Bergers d'Arcadie, c.1637. Seen High Museum of Art, Atlanta 22/03/07)

if only
the Example
helped

      if only the
dumb
Shepherds weren't
so dim

      so
stunted
by Environment

tracing the hole
in R
Eternally

*

game dame
Memory   her
nose hypotenuse
her hand
on hip   Imparting this
harsh truth
a hundredth Time

her
other
resting

on his back   as
though
Drunk

*

impractical robes and
Dainty sandals   trio
of sticks
suggesting
Evening   has
come early

*

(death's
heritage Endures   his
victims'
not
so much)

*

            so
'paused
to Focus'   where
can they
go now?

            perhaps
they will
Forget

Rob Stanton

Hammershøiku

(Vilhelm Hammershøi, 1864-1916)

One door. Another.
Does this blank room intend to
Blanket or smother?

*

A woman, back turned.
His tempo doesn't bother
Hers. A patience, earned.

*

I don't pretend to
Understand what can't be learned.
Reserves I tend to.

Three States

1.

Wherever our leader's
Attention leans, there's
The centre. The army a jewel he
Carries with him. The people cheer.
The wheat fields. Our enemies gather at
The circumference (the light is blinding there, fully corrosive).

2.

Words, numbers list the orders
Here. Our leader speaks to God and
Lets us know. The army is invisible
And terrible. God loves his people, builds
Walls from our bones. Our enemy
Is far away, beyond the sea, yet drawing close.

3.

Our leader a fond memento
Of what leaders meant. The army a
Tolerated pit-bull. Our enemy
Everywhere and nowhere. People mock
Themselves, the army, enemy, all
Endeavour, yet their will is law, or near to.

Rob Stanton

Over It

Psychotherapy's
last gasp; the autumn sidewalk's
thin regret of snow.

III. Sequences, 2005 - 2010

Bresson: *L'Argent*
(for Colin Winborn)

'To make what you see
be seen, through the intermediacy of a machine
that does not see it as you see it.'

1. 'Make people diviners. Make them desire it.'

notes

to

ward

money

some failed

or

Doors make prisons. Doors
possible. Necessary. Doors
Prison

make prisons
make prisons

2. 'Empty the pond to get the fish.'

money's

as contagious
as

and/or
both

(for
bother both

what isn't

what hasn't

get

more   in

3. 'The eye (in general) superficial, the ear profound and inventive.
A locomotive's whistle imprints in us a whole railroad station.'

the traffic

noise

passing?

the
hand's

      trans-
action

the
body

porn

is beautiful

Hand. Money. Hand. Money.

The traffic

Ha

4. *'Model who, in spite of himself and you,* frees the real man from the fictitious man you had imagined.'

a few
seconds
to register
then   "I'll
pass it on"

denial a simple
shake – very slight –
of the head

WORK DETAIL:

Machine. Attendant
Nozzle. Funnel
Gloves

5. 'Make the objects look as if they want to be there.'

in

the
dark-

room

"I'll be
kinder

when I'm rich"

film   'lies'
in
boxes

money
buys

quiet

one

6. 'Cutting. Phosphorus that wells up suddenly from your models, floats around them and binds them to the objects (blue of Cézanne, grey of El Greco).'

seen
as a pulling
toward (grasp)
and a thrusting
away (release). A
hand

Confrontation

palm open

fingers
splayed

Table-
cloth   falls
in stages

'small-

timers'   who

'handle'

7. 'Shooting. Agony of making sure not to let slip any part of what I merely glimpse, of what I perhaps do not yet see and shall only later be able to see.'

the
map
collapsed

no   need
of a key

urgency: the
other way

slow mo

echoes

of whistles

& shots

denial of

presence

madness

back
up to   investigate

hands
grip the wheel

foot seeks
acceleration

8. 'Several takes of the same thing, like a painter who does several pictures or drawings of the same subject and, each fresh time, *progresses toward rightness.'*

death
of innocence as
much (or
little) a matter
as   the
opening & closing
of a door

lowered
hand
guides the

child through
a double
threshold

see-
through
Door
versus
non-
see-through
door

Down
the stairs
and hard
across
the floor

9. 'The omnipotence of rhythms. Nothing is durable but what is caught up in rhythms. Bend content to form and sense to rhythms.'

the
whole
rigmarole

lousy
with exits

exchange

becomes

commodity

an
(empty)
van

terrible
news

in   piles

kids   as

witnesses

10. 'Quality of a new world which none of the existing cuts allowed to be imagined.'

com-
pose your
new
code

                     fool

the device

crook

liar

the immense

giver

ENTER YOUR
CODE

TAKE YOUR

corridor

in the

Metro

MONEY

CARD

guilt passes

11. 'Model. You illumine him and he illumines you. The light you receive from him is added to the light he receives from you.'

a grabbed
& futile
instrument

will
reduced to the
scraping of
a metal bowl
a-
cross a
floor

rebel
more

    simply

      not
   that door

        new
        vehicle

       a similar
       rigmarole

take

another
        hand-
out
       refused

12. 'These horrible days – when shooting film disgusts me, when I am exhausted, powerless in the face of so many obstacles – are part of my method of work.'

you

eventually

are free

       at
the Hotel
Moderne everything looks
this way

(red a
bad sign

spoils   balanced

            even

one final

swish round
the register

13. 'Do not draw back from prodigies. Command the moon, the sun. Let loose the thunder and the lightning.'

exact &
meaningful
ritual

mad fool

across bridge

amid green

followed the way

angry ghost

(losing his pupils

damp patch where
the glass
fell

taken care of

for   a reason   for

        forgiveness

axe awaits

amid the hay

14. 'To TRANSLATE the invisible wind by the water it sculpts in passing.'

a couple
of minutes

one
last
drink

the ripples
subside

that's
that

you were holding
your breath

15. 'The terrible habit of theatre.'

has

us

where

he

placed

to

witness

this?

16. 'The faculty of using my resources well diminishes when their number grows.'

what

are they
coming

for

from

absence
of answer
won't help
stop onlookers

"where's

the   money?"

no other
ending possible: the
'pay off' and
the walk out

"where's

the money

opened doors
awaken space
to us

Wells: I, II, III

I.i

Dawn is not
what she was

*

Wars & illness
make the most

*

Each of her
books is one

*

A ghost tormented
by further ghosts

*

Bowls & dishes
such as us

*

All that is
hard & fast

I.ii

Creating autonomous atmosphere
a long game

*

Trail its own
pursuit of happiness

*

This afternoon everyone
is an official

*

Taking a good
lead in following

*

Making good time
taking your own

*

All snug aboard
the wasting snow

I.iii

With little (or
no) attention span

*

Another poor motive
seeps into view

*

Broad daylight manoeuvres
mean to end

*

From one car
to the next

*

Coming to fatigue
by every route

*

Pet to prophet
in one gear-change

II.i

I wrote a
brand new wagon

*

I get to
keep this part

*

I feel appropriately
challenged & supported

*

I was comfortable
not knowing that

*

I surfed a
sea of surfaces

*

I am, admit
it, liar

II.ii

Cannot wonder at
my withdrawing myself

*

These marshals positioned
round the room

*

Sly un-precious passage
out of sleep

*

Feed the dead
on scrambled eggs

*

Compel an existing
individual to exist

*

Whole lobster-pots full
of non-discrete conclusion

II.iii

The future doesn't
exist in English

*

Who has seen
the target page?

*

Who expects to
do what portal?

*

Credit it elastic
enough to fit

*

What could such
a one expect?

*

Mute worry &
the threshing-floor beforehand

III.i

Vocation to vacation
from the outset

*

Moved & moved
& moved again

*

Levels thought through
as you entered

*

A frustrating 'Mediterranean'
of the interior

*

Tread the very
outskirts of empire

*

Amply & freely
spread the butter

Rob Stanton

III.ii

Floods his system
with over-the-top adrenalin

*

Regards himself a
guinea pig perhaps

*

Pallor often seen
when under threat

*

Zero interest in
being a person

*

Looking to himself
as looked at

*

Never so becoming
as right now

III.iii

Last day of
the dog days

*

This used wristwatch's
second-hand second hand

*

Venture to appear
as frankness itself

*

Moon & you
up all night

*

Mind jolts out
of deep relaxation

*

*I need to
go to sleep*

Rob Stanton

The Middle's
'Pinnacled dim in the intense inane.'

'Turns out many of our shared concerns are identical.'

1. **'PREOCCUPATION.** Is active and fruitful in proportion to one's immobility, which in turn is caused by the depth of one's absorption.'

My cubicle
Is not

My own,
More palimpsest

Of local
Timed occupancies,

Mine being
Now. The

Air is
Burning outdoors.

(Here's no
Such flare.)

2. **'COMFORT.** The most valuable discovery of modern times.'

Our brisk,	(Salad &
Crisp lives	One fruit).

Artists observable
Under glass

World's biggest
Manmade lake

The panic	(Sea oversees
Room remembered.	Its dotage.)

3. 'TRAVELLING. Should be by the fastest means.'

Asocial, I
Ricochet slowly

Round a
Fixed domain

Habitat of
Some iconoclast

Not me.
All the

Incoming onlookers
Want out.

All chairs
Stand empty.

4. 'ARCHITECTS. All idiots: they always forget to put in the stairs.'

Part – Orphic   Our 'ongoing'
Orifice – of   Promotion, our

Corporate interior
Pantomimes time's

Renewal (the
Foyer's plastic

Shrub offsets   Both compliment
The carpet;   The woodwork).

5. TIME (OUR). Thunder against. Lament the fact that it is not poetical. Call it a time of transition, of decadence.'

Rituals are
Usually tamer.

Another Friday
Drones on.

(*Meme me,*
Search engine . . .

Did I
Drop off?)

Deftly as
They come

My purposes
Stay staid.

6. 'CROCODILE. Imitates the cry of a child to lure men.'

Checking my
Profile online

I imagine
My workplace

Exactly as
It is.

(& we
– *Like sheep!* –

& we
– *Like sheep!* –

Have turned
& fled).

7. 'CONSPIRATORS. They feel a compulsion to write down their names on a list.'

Capital eats   *My hurt.*
My heart   The same

Damned platitudes
Erupting everywhere.

I deny
Having seen

The man   I deny
In question.   Having seen.

8. **'CHILDREN.** Give signs of a passionate attachment to all children when others are looking on.'

Secret Santa.
Round Robin.

The stories
We tell

Our children
Redistribute care

Evenly. The
Circuitry gets

Smaller. Smarter.
Embedded. We,

Within, threaten
To evaporate.

9. **'IMPORTS.** Canker at the heart of trade.'

Our aim
In labour

Echoing off
The near.

I lie,
I lied.

Supply &
Demand &

(On the
Other hand)

What we
Actually require.

10. **'HOSTILITIES.** Hostilities are like oysters, they have to be opened. "Open hostilities" sounds as if one ought to sit down at table.'

What I
Really want?

We – *THE*
PEOPLE – shall

Decide. (Deicide?
Regicide? Recycled

Reprisal of
What flagged

Aria? 'Area'
To be

'Redeemed'? What
Tacit approval?)

11. **'ARISTOCRACY.** Despise and envy it.'

Take care   Wandered off
Walking home.   Eleven year.

                                   I need
                                   My rightful

                                   Crown – &
                                   Agony – restored.

Outcry of   (Mercury's memory's
Doubtful lineage.   Sieved, dammed.)

12. 'METHOD. Of no use whatever.'

Physician un-   Desk to
To physics –   Desk to

Parking-lot – my
Eye embraces

The harmony
I perceive.

(Welcome to   The weariness.
The occupation.   The will.)

13. 'SEA. Bottomless. Symbol of infinity. Induces deep thoughts. At the shore one should always have a good glass. While contemplating the sea, always exclaim: "Water, water everywhere."'

Here is   & who
The sea   Shall drain

                                 It dry?
                                 The eye

                                 Unhinges itself
                                 Taking it

All in.   Again the
Again &   Shutters stutter.

14. 'MOON. Induces melancholy. May be inhabited.'

This is   Somewhere in
Your station.   (Or on)

Laughable birdcall
Feigns normality.

Last one
Home a-

Drift in   ('Station'? I
Pooled fluorescence.   Meant 'terminal' ...)

15. 'DOMESTICITY. Never fail to speak of it with respect.'

Night leaks
Through cracks

Usually friendly
By day

(That *pet*
In *repetition*).

We live
Near ambulances:

Sirens slam
Me awake.

I fumble
For agenda.

16. **'ANT.** Model to cite in front of a spendthrift. Suggested the idea of savings banks.'

You won't   (Anybody could
See me.   Shoot anybody:

Arm yourself
For peace.)

The international
Blank seems

Less &   More &
Less compelling,   More untried.

17. **'DIPLOMACY.** A distinguished career, but beset with difficulties and full of mystery. Suited only to aristocrats. A profession of vague import, though higher than trade. Diplomats are invariably subtle and shrewd.'

A city   A village
Implies solitude,   A hostage.

Office gossip
Had me

Standoffish. Obtuse.
(Are you

A being   To good
Wholly receptive   Or evil?)

18. 'COUNTRY. People in the country better than those in towns. Envy their lot. In the country, anything goes – sloppy clothes, practical jokes, etc.'

Love only   (Morning air –
Resurgent spring.   Bluer, brighter,

Less resistant:
The general

Population yet
To make

Their appearance.   Autumn downfall
Time delegates.)   Only love.

19. 'BUREAUCRAT. Inspires awe, no matter what bureau he works in.'

Placed here

– A bookmark –

I shuffle

Uneasily amid

Papers strewn.

What to

Do with

No window?

Expound/explode/

excommunicate/exfoliate?

Given everything,

Want more.

20. 'STOICISM. Not feasible.'

Water over-   Rain proves
Lapping roof: Itself anterior,

Auteur. Fish-food
Partially drunk.

An a
Priori system

Nonsense. 'Get   Flume a
Off here':   'Distinguished' exit.

21. **'ASSASSIN.** Always a coward, even when he acted with daring and courage. Yet less reprehensible than a firebug.'

Carbonated; carbon-
Dated; calcified.

Was me.
Is now

Upgraded (soft-
Ware hard-

Wired – simultaneously
Sluggish &

Upbeat). Having
Real trouble

Observing gravity's
Insoluble levity ...

22. **'AGRICULTURE.** One of the two nourishing breasts of the state (the state is masculine, but never mind). Should be encouraged. Short of hands.'

I see   Ache up.
Plots. Marigolds   Sun giver

Then despoiler.
How could

Anyone handle
The sheer

Incoherence of   *Small patch*
Even a   *Of earth?*

23. 'INSTRUMENT. If used to commit a crime, always "blunt" – unless it happens to be sharp.'

Not yet
Us, I

Procrastinate. Try
To pretend

To fret.
Retreat down

Prosperity Drive.
Push my

Headphones further
In. Idealise

Grasses' strong
Individual blades.

24. **'PROSPECTS.** Find them beautiful in nature, dark in politics.'

Nothing is   (Less lesson,

That individual   More morsel).

Aspire to

Effect a

Sideways getaway.

The windows

Here prove   Nothing need

Intensely clear.   Be found.

Rob Stanton

Wells: IV, V, VI

IV.i

Mirror neurons seize
the pre-frontal cortex

*

Hitting him directly
in the forehead

*

Sloppily-painted squares as
soul's X-rayed intentions

*

Salt your wounds
& earth alike

*

Dung beetle flits
about its load

*

A push. A
start. A package

IV.ii

Sliver dust in;
golden dust out

*

To know means
to know means

*

NO HIDDEN WEAPONRY
PAST THIS POINT

*

End not an
end in itself

*

USE SEAT BOTTOM
CUSHION FOR FLOATATION

*

*Fuck this shit
up yr arse*

IV.iii

Get out of
here before I

*

An abyss, with
birds in it

*

Eyes rise up
& down day

*

Right: fresh creation;
Left: false memory

*

Sensory impulse router
To cortex, amygdala

*

Comfort zone on
edge, accelerating, bereft

V.i

Father 'something devious'
in the city

*

Three wreaths adorn
the non-descript side-street

*

Attempted grief as
circular & template

*

God continues breathing
when he shouldn't

*

Juries & other
imponderable communities swayed

*

Error on error
stumps to righteousness

V.ii

I am ideal
in your deployment

*

King of no
normal kingdom retrieved

*

Relief at what
a number come

*

Quick mental representative
takes a spin

*

Converted, later on,
into a tool

*

Dance, at one
remove from dance-floor

V.iii

Playing the man
like an instrument

*

Chewing away at
the obvious resonance

*

Complicates the listening
of the tribe

*

Doing the obvious
in different voices

*

Ever be so
cruel to me

*

Sit tight &
let time come

VI.i

Time a predictable
fire, viewed again

*

Describing architecture/strata/
species of cloud

*

*Each shadow a
reproach to sun*

*

Tensed as if
water rushed in

*

Here where the
clowns came to

*

Incessant rhythmic sunlight
not so common

VI.ii

Here is where
you 'glimpsed' Eden

*

The Technicolor plunge
with words discernible

*

Wit & its
blunt counterpoint converge

*

Some day I'll
outsmart this wall

*

Window as a
menu to impatience

*

Throw a rock,
part a sea

VI.iii

Look at that
building they're building

*

Recourse to resources
not yet born

*

Drawing & redrawing
you his pain

*

Fun cross between
scripture & sculpture

*

Sleep sleep of
the just denounced

*

Storm in a
teacup breaks teacup

Buildings

i.

This: the opening of an ongoing
Attempt, undertaken at (I hope) not
Quite midway, to render up that ever-
Elusive 'true account'. What (if anything)
Do I believe in? I love my wife, my
Family, friends. I like most people I
Encounter, despite myself and (sometimes)
Them. Look Mum, no hands. What else do I have?

ii.

Now (looking down) I see I have written
Exactly what I would have done. I have
No childhood scars, except those craters – tiny,
Shallow – left by chickenpox (a bad case,
I'm told, though I wonder: maybe I
Just itched). Resentment, either way, did not cross
My path until much later. Maybe I
Con myself in this, but I don't think so.

iii.

The repeatability of a name
Endlessly strange – *stolen away from a*
Place of stone – and strangely detachable,
As though applicable to someone else
Also living my life. The Cotswold town
My family descended upon each
Summer to collect our 'tithes'. Just harmless
Fun. Car sickness oddly comforting.

iv.

No interest at all in keeping a
Diary/score. I've always wanted to float
Above, devoid of biography, a
Nerveless eye. *Yes* to sensual body, *yes*
To accruing experience, knowledge, but
No to performing personality, the
Roll-call of expected behaviour, the
Conspiracy of total presence/soul.

v.

'Harmless' because unspoken? Butterflies
Flit (ardent ceremonies we a-
Lone can see as such – one swallow in fact
Making a summer). On the other hand, the
Vagaries of so-called holidays: I see
Another reminisce another
Let-down one feels 'greater' to have faced.
Our 'tithes' made up of lunch bought in a pub.

vi.

My first memory consists of having
Dirt under my fingernails; a fleet of
Die-cast cars on a tilted driveway; a house
I no longer remember the interior
Of (one vague flash: of a dining-room – my
Mother's parents there); a short set of steps
Down to a lawn. Overturned stones from a rock-
Garden yielding woodlice, damp. Ants stirred up, then drowned.

vii.

Toy soldiers organized into a raid –
Plastic yet inflexible – an unyielding
Range of roles (the general in me liked conformity,
The human varied – I simply assumed an
Otherness my own [– *who doesn't?*]). Fostered
In calm, I wonder: was I anxious? Fear
Has been a constant since, awareness that keeping
Schtum deflects trouble. Or attracts it. A bind.

viii.

Slowly introduced to history, the 'soul'
Feels encumbered by a 'joy'
It can scarcely gainsay – there are no hills
To picture it from. The regal bric-a-brac
Of fused estates, cities displaying fixed
Hierarchies like rings in a cross-sectioned
Tree. Playgrounds of us kids preparing for
Whatever future the past excretes us into.

ix.

A horde of treasured phrases not a haul
Another would see the point of necessarily
(Perhaps another shares a few choice cuts
And friendship can be forged from matching halves).
But 'taste' is all about amassing more
Of something the majority desires
Before it knows it needs it. Light a-
Cross an otherwise static landscape.

x.

Mind slinks ways the conscious will can only
Follow/intimate/suggest … I don't want that
To put me off. Laws may be immutable, but I –
Even if they prove too prolix to
Be grasped – I want to try. Predatory
In its intentions, imagination
Leaps to extremes – infernos, cataracts – no mere
Matters to be parsed into a letter …

xi.

There was enough of everything for all.
In my dream, that is. There was also a terrible
Conflict coming (make of that what you will). A
Ear-splitting Hollywood explosion on the soundtrack pre-
Lude to complete annihilation. I
Woke up glad. To be awake, that is. A
Day assembled. A later realisation:
There is enough of everything for all.

xii.

No-one or nothing to thank for being born
In – such sheer luck – comfort and ease, I contemplate
Jackals in business suits who push the buttons,
The multitudes who suffer, bearing
The consequences. No comeback or feedback
Allowed: hindsight and overview are 'luxuries'
We cannot afford. We need them. The
Face beneath the hood a mystery.

xiii.

Least (ha ha) among them? Who (or what) most
Move me? Socrates, beseeching Athens to
Raise his sons as he would – doubtful, alert –
Knowing they would not? Celan, writing
A single word – *Stehend* – on a postcard?
Sebald? Tennyson? David Foster Wallace?
Self-lost, or lost. Sappho? Dickinson? The
Countless anonymous corpses underground?

xiv.

Over grass, beneath the same vast bill-
Board every day (the other rigged to
Scroll through several options; this one
Professes education at another location
Not nearby). Promotion of due betterment a
Lie, to some degree – hard work no guarantee of
Pay-off, shallow roots sustained (to date)
In shifting soil – indeed, in a swamp.

xv.

Pieced together only gradually: love
Of reading, words – carved out of solitude, yet
Not its cause (*that* may stand forever un-
Explained, even to myself – a chipped tooth the
Tongue explores, but cautiously, as though to
Tease out pain, repeat it, have it linger …).
Forgotten, then remembered, weirdly, later,
'Vocation' not an option. A re-calling.

xvi.

Terrible handwriting: notes from two
Weeks back already indecipherable.
Cultivating a signature, I over-
Look my shortcomings: clarity its
Own reward. Fraught tendernesses for
Spaces I have written in, at least in
Theory/memory. After I left they
Planned to knock it through. Access denied.

xvii.

Gravity as reminder. Gardens make
Me uneasy, temporary stays. I
Feel guilty for not loving nature more
Or for itself. Humanity my measure,
More or less, despite a lack of winning
Evidence, myself included. One of the few
Things we do beyond bare necessity, art. Its having
No 'value' its greatest asset. It's still earth-bound.

xviii.

Translation as metaphor? It's poetry
Itself, getting one over. I can't speak
For anyone else or in another tongue.
Conscious, cutting in, of a lack of
'Personal content', I take my place in words in-
Stead. Arrange them how I will, the facts
Remain: I want to reach through them to get to
You. *Communion abasement on all fronts.*

xix.

Car radio here another beast entirely: a
Procession of different eras, decades,
Hits – alternative history a blast
From the past (one hopes) and not some looming future
Of greater confinement. What to think
Between trips to the mall, the store, the bank?
That *I am here*, a man unloading things
Out of his car, to place them in his home.

xx.

Folly of the folly of philosophy
Useful regardless. I looked in briefly then
Turned away, trusting to a sea of the
Superfluous instead. Not there yet. Not
Here, exactly, either. Lecture hall a
Bad correlative. Pub, maybe: late
Afternoon, everybody friends, talk allowed to
Drift, as it desires, to relevant depths.

xxi.

Folly embraced as consolation
Not everyone can take in. Evolution
Sets you back: the counter-intuitive teeth-
Array of the angler-fish not, surprisingly,
Impossible. Behind the immediate problem
Lies a deeper, original
Flaw. No-one can solve it: *burn it down*.
The residue of bonfires acrid, tasty.

xxii.

Watching from the window early (or late),
Rabbits in the field opposite, imagining the
Cold anxiety within the seemingly
Idyllic: the constant fight for food or for
The right to procreate. Exhausting. I
Needed to get out of there, to find another
Way. I think I did. Now, living honestly,
I see those rabbits in a whole new light.

xxiii.

Hey, festivities deaden me: I
Prefer, sadly, those moments of minor quiet,
Lightenings unprepared for and (as such)
Not quite believed in. That said, *let's party!* – beggars
Can't be choosers; a tidy retinue is all
I crave. Apart from that, freedom and the space
To keep on keeping on. Hey, that's a
Cliché! Fair cop. A sleeping dog. A horse to water.

xxiv.

A shared emphatic photograph misplaced then re-
Discovered, later, behind the desk and
Pondered anew. Safety of *in here* contrasted to
The thrill of *out there* – promises of
Experiment/experience. What happened? I let myself
Shrink. For a while, I hope. Now: the business
Of bursting out afresh. We'll see. Stories
I told myself prove somewhat useful.

xxv.

Transported on the spot by a displacement
Itself sublime – brick by brick, block by block – and re-
Assembled here in a gleaming
More-or-less Modernist shell. Let's
Not kid ourselves: *Capital Rules.* This was a
Site of ritual belief and it is still.
Self-lost in The Ramble, on the way, a gloomy
Dappled 'wood' a more salubrious haunt indeed.

xxvi.

An easy transposition of up and down,
Seemingly. Wake & work, and do it
With a secret inner peace, despite surface
Tension, irritations, matters to be
Resolved. Shift gears with nary a twinge
Of muscular adjustment. What *is* this to
Have walked into? Don't doubt it or it
May evaporate, just as you suspect.

xxvii.

Must I adopt a pattern from the past,
Base myself on forebears I don't know, or
Take my father's bedrock decency as
Only model? My writer-grandfather,
On holiday, stubbornly finding the
Plaka agora a happy hunting ground?
I'd like to be, like him, up to the end,
A democrat, a wise man and a fool.

xxviii.

No: my own man, me. (Whatever that means.) I
Worry that some strings are better hidden,
That every choice we make can be predicted. *I*
An other. How 'deranged' can it become
And still make sense? 'Accessible' not a
Buzz-word I like; I do find exhibition dis-
Tasteful, though can't deny the expressionistic
Urge, pigment-splattered, wordless in its rage.

xxix.

This will be our litmus test: will I, in
Thirty odd years, still qualify, or
Will I have spurned it all, be bitter, shriveled
Up? Where to look for lasting sweetnesses?
Rooting for blackberries, family
Around and somewhere near, investigating other
Branches, bushes. Ambivalent rewards of toil
Sweet-bitter, sometimes worm-infested, worthy.

XXX.

My America, American. A term
Of absence *and* endearment, time to stop
Wool-gathering and moss-gathering: *we are on*
Our way. Where to? Good question, but not
(Apparently) as central or as vital as who's
The company kept. *Incomparable*
Thank you the reply. To you, my love, my
Word. To everybody else: Bon voyage. Write me.

xxxi.

Lightning like I'd never seen before, rain
Dense and drenching – afraid of the weather in
Whole new ways: flash-floods, hurricanes, tornadoes –
Speed-damage on inhuman scales. *Wow*
My watchword. Fresh territory on top
Of race, religion, regional bias: things to learn, not
Necessarily to accept. Longing to absorb
Both highs and lows, the famous sun, the rain.

xxxii.

Out in that rain, and glad I am not porous, I
Consider the cost of a protracted
Stay. The presence of my loved one as a
Bridge (*halo of other loved ones' light, hello*).
Made out of – in the dim and distant – mud,
I don't fear death (abstracted). I fear
Pain, senility, absence, coma. I
Don't want life to outlive memory.